The Top

Written by Abie Longstaff

Collins

Pack a mat.

Pack a cap.

Pack a gas can.

Pack a tin and a pot.

the kit

a map

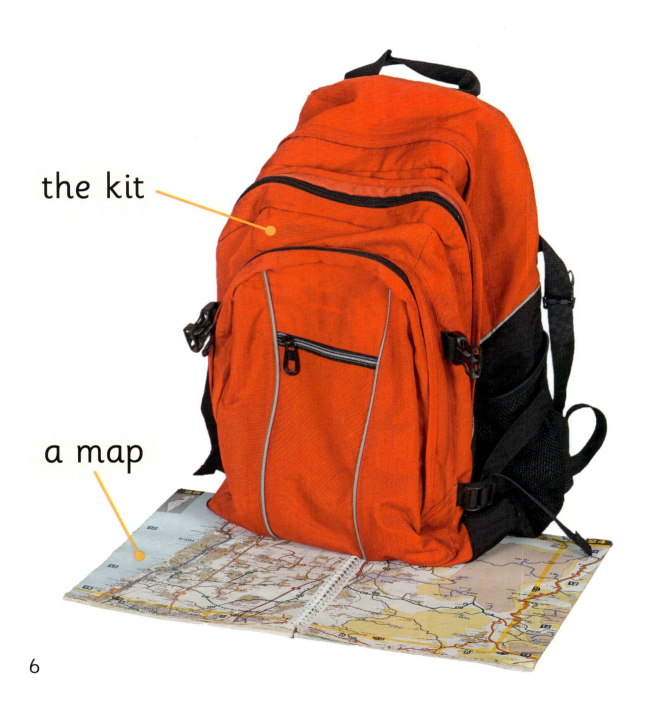

Is the top on the map?

The dot is the top.

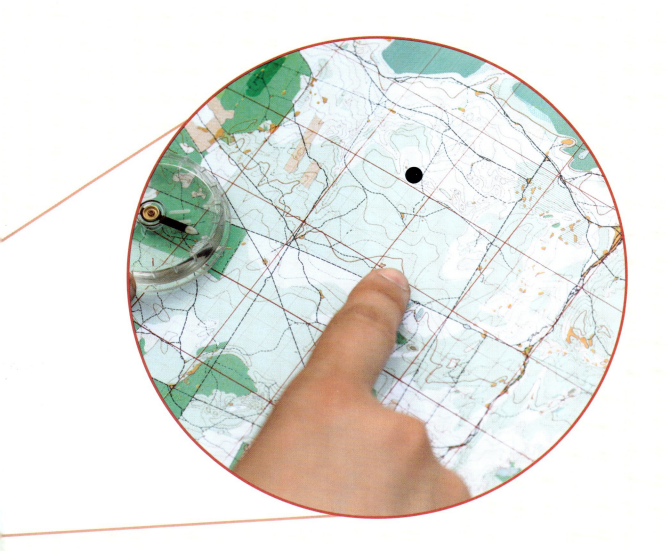

at the top

Sit on a mat.

A pot is on the gas can.

a tin

13

14

15

 Review: After reading

Use your assessment from hearing the children read to choose any GPCs, words or tricky words that need additional practice.

Read 1: Decoding

- Read page 12. To check the children's understanding, ask the children to point to the **pot** and then the **gas can**. Talk about how the gas can is used to heat the pot.
- Point to **kit** on page 6, allowing the children to sound and blend out loud. Turn back to page 3, and encourage them to blend in their heads, silently, before reading the words aloud. Ask: Which letter and letters make the same /c/ sound? (*"c" and "k" in pack, "c" in cap*)
- Look at the "I spy sounds" pages (14–15) together. Point to the tomatoes, and say "tomato", emphasising the /t/ sound. Ask the children to find other items in the picture that start with the /t/ sound. (e.g. *tree, top, tiger, train, tissue, torch, tea, tent, tennis ball*) Point to the oranges, and say "orange", emphasising the /o/ sound. Ask the children to find other items in the picture that start with the /o/ sound. (e.g. *olives, octopus, orange clothes*)

Read 2: Prosody

- Focus on the question mark.
  - Model reading the question on page 8. Ask the children: How do I know this is a question? (*the question mark*) Encourage the children to read the sentence in a questioning voice.
  - Ask the children to read page 9, pointing out how this is the answer and just ends in a full stop. Check they read the sentence in an answering voice.

Read 3: Comprehension

- Encourage the children to talk about any outdoor trips they have experienced or seen. Ask: Did you or the people you saw go to the top of something? What did they take with them?
- Talk about the things that the man and boy took. Ask:
  - On page 5, why did they pack a tin and a pot? (e.g. *so they could cook on their trip*)
  - On pages 8 and 9, what did they use the map for? (e.g. *to find the top of the hill*)
- Turn to pages 12 and 13. Ask: Why did the man and boy eat a meal outside? Discuss how people might need to cook meals when they are on long walks or on a camping trip.